DID YOU HEAR WHAT I SAID?

Mastering the Underemphasized Side of Communication

HOW TO BECOME A 100% LISTENER

10 POWERFUL TOOLS
TO IMPROVE YOUR LISTENING EFFECTIVENESS

Olin R. Jennings and Laura N. Jennings

Published by:

The Jennings Group, LLC
www.TheJenningsGroup.com

TABLE OF CONTENTS

This book is dedicated to all of the students and participants in our training programs - from whom we have learned so much.

1. LISTENING – THE UNDEREMPHASIZED PART OF COMMUNICATION

Many people never give listening much thought and really don't recognize its full value. We all know and talk about the need for good communication. What we overlook is the importance of listening in good communication. Listening is the underemphasized side of communication. Good communication is like a good football pass. The communication pass must be thrown well, but it has to be caught to be of any value. Listening is the art of catching the communication pass.

Are you an effective listener, a 100% listener? Many of us lack some of the skills needed to be effective listeners *or* we can improve the skills that we have. We are not aware of what we are missing with our bad listening habits.

Even if *we* are good listeners, many of the people around us need to improve *their* listening – subordinates, co-workers, friends, and family members. An understanding of the 10 listening tools in this book will equip you and others to grow as listeners.

This book summarizes what we have learned in our research and our training programs about how to become a 100% listener. It was written as a short, practical guide with four objectives:

1. Test your listening skills;
2. Help you understand how you listen;
3. Give you a more systematic way to think about listening;
4. Give you practical tools to help you improve your listening skills.

This book is a guide to good listening practices and contains 10 powerful listening tools. It also is a personal workbook to help you build these skills and give you a personal plan for improving your listening over time. Therefore, as you read the chapters, please do the exercises to test your listening skills and abilities. Think about what you are learning personally about yourself and your listening. Think about how you, personally, can grow your listening skills.

The 10 Listening Tools

1. Being fully present (Chapter 8)
2. Controlled verbal and mental response (Chapter 9 and 10)
3. Listening specifically to word choice (Chapter 11)
4. Reading meaning from tone and inflection (Chapter 12)
5. Listening without words – reading body language (Chapter 13)
6. Confirmation (Chapter 14)
7. Empathetic listening (Chapter 15 and 16)
8. Eye contact when talking (Chapter 17)
9. Using your body to be a better listener (Chapter 18)
10. Using a translator to take the sting out of words (Chapter 19)

Congratulations on recognizing the importance of listening in effective communication. We promise you improved listening skills and greater success in interacting with the people in your life.

2. WE ARE A NATION OF INCOMPLETE LISTENERS

Do you sometimes have a sense that you were listening, but didn't really hear what was said? Or are listening, but don't understand what the other person is really trying to say? Or, you are talking and just know that the other person is not connecting. We all experience these feelings, sometimes more often than we would like. Why does this happen?

We are a nation of incomplete listeners. We are a nation that is constantly on the move, constantly trying to listen and do other things at the same time. We often hear comments like:

"It's just more effective to listen while I'm doing other things."

or

"How will I get everything done if I have to take the time to stop and listen?"

or

"I know that you're talking, but how important can it really be?"

These rationales for incomplete listening sound absurd if we stop to think about what we really are saying. But this is what we think and what we do too often. What's your excuse for being an incomplete listener? Since life has less conflict and better relationships if we improve our communication, how rational is *your* excuse?

One of our daughters went to Outward Bound's mountaineering course and carried her "relaxed" listening style with her. These programs build confidence by putting participants in leadership positions. The instructor gave directions for the day and pronounced our daughter as the day's leader. Off she led with her partially heard directions. Early afternoon found them on the wrong side of the mountain with most of the group in open revolt and arguing over where they were supposed to be.

Another example comes to mind from a senior manager:

> "Yesterday, I was pressed to get to a meeting and was intercepted by my one of my managers with a question about a project. I didn't have the time to give her my full attention and really listen. I cut her off, made some assumptions about what she was going to say, and gave her an answer. Today, she showed up in my office all upset because she was convinced that I didn't value her as a manager and didn't respect her as a person, and so on. I had to spend 30 minutes with her to fix the problem I created yesterday while saving 3 minutes."

But it's not just time pressures. Sometimes we are under stress or in conflict. Sometimes, we just know that we are right and are more interested in proving our own point than in listening to what the other person is saying.

Sometimes, we don't respect the other person or his/her ideas. When we are dismissive in listening, we are less able to hear and really understand. There are regional, cultural, and gender differences that affect our understanding as we listen. At times our strong will gets in the way. Sometimes we are demotivated or a little burned out. And the list goes on and on.

Does this sound a little too familiar? Welcome to the Listening Problems Club! We all have examples of incomplete listening in every part of our lives. Listening problems take place everywhere. They are in our jobs between bosses and subordinates, between co-workers, between project team members, and between customers and suppliers. They are everywhere in the rest of our lives as well – between husbands and wives, between significant others, between siblings, between friends, and between adults and children.

What happens when we are incomplete listeners? We may find that we have an incomplete understanding of what we need to be doing – in getting to the right side of the mountain, in relationships, in tasks, in our jobs, and in other parts of our lives. The other people may feel that their ideas were not considered, or may feel slighted or not receiving the respect they are due (and long for). Listening problems contribute to unnecessary conflict and stress, lost sales, being in the wrong place at the wrong time, poor quality or poor performance, tasks that must be redone, lost time, poor self-esteem, and more.

But we already know these things about listening and ourselves. We all would like to improve and be more effective communicators. The purpose of this book is to help you recognize the subtleties of good listening and answer the question, "How can we become 100% listeners?". This book will help you understand how you listen. The worksheets will test your listening skills and give you a benchmark for improvement. This book will give you a more systematic way to think about listening. It will show you how to use 10 powerful listening tools that will help you improve your listening skills over time.

3. WHY SHOULD WE TRY TO IMPROVE OUR LISTENING?
(Why *really* listening is important)

On a day-to-day basis, we all listen, but most of us don't think too much about *how* we are listening. So, it makes sense to spend a minute or two on why *really* listening is important in every part of our lives. Our reasons for listening are as real and as varied as the range of life experiences that we go through each day. But the bottom line is that part of growing our emotional intelligence is understanding how we listen and finding ways to improve our listening.

The most important reason for good listening is that *really* listening shows the other person that you have respect for them – that they matter as a person and that they matter to you personally. Why is this important? Nothing stops or diverts unwarranted conflict faster or more effectively than genuine respect for the other person. More on this later.

Other reasons for listening relate to the essential ingredients of being more effective in any situation involving personal interactions, as well as being an effective manager or leader in any environment – work, home, community, church, etc. Regardless of what we think, we generally don't have all of the answers or all of the information that we need. We need to depend on others. *Really* listening helps us to:

- Get information necessary to know how best to get into action, help others, or get the right answer;

- Understand points of difference and be more effective in building consensus and agreement;

- Understand better where the other person is coming from and avoid unnecessary or unwarranted stress and conflict;

- Be more effective in resolving conflict to get win-win results by understanding issues or points of disagreement;

- Understand what is truly important to someone and be more effective in motivating them;

- Understand points or issues when initiating change and be more effective in creating positive environments for change;

- Understand what is *not* being said, so that we are in a better position to draw out the unspoken meaning or ask for additional information;

- Understand better the potential risks in a given situation and be more comfortable in taking personal or career risk and then controlling that risk.

This is not an all-inclusive list, but it is a starting place for you to think about your own situations and experiences, and to understand and develop reasons for listening that are personal and meaningful to you.

We believe that people learn, grow, and improve best when they can personally relate to the subject. In other words, "it matters to me personally in my life". To make the rest of this book more relevant to you personally, take five or ten minutes to think about your work situation, personal life, relationships, and family. Also, think about some of the stresses or conflicts in your life. How much have your listening skills helped you or contributed to problems.

First, think of situations in which incomplete listening complicated your life or where incomplete listening resulted in an undesired outcome.

RESULTS OF MY INCOMPLETE LISTENING

Now think of situations in which someone else did not listen to you completely and where their incomplete listening resulted in an undesired outcome

RESULTS OF INCOMPLETE LISTENING BY OTHERS

The authors have found significant benefits in becoming better listeners in business, as consultants and trainers, as well as in our personal lives. The "what's the point" or reason it matters to us personally is the tangible benefit we get when we are more effective listeners – things like:

- Less misunderstanding in conversations;
- Less conflict created by misunderstanding the other person;
- More effective responses – we understand what the other person meant;
- Less "do over" work;
- Time savings – communication can be quicker if we wish;
- Better interpersonal relationships because people believe we respect them and care about them;
- Greater sense of success and better self image for ourselves – we get better results.

Now it's your turn. Make a list of five or six reasons for becoming a better listener – reasons that matter to you personally.

	MY PERSONAL REASONS FOR IMPROVING MY LISTENING SKILLS ("Why it matters to me personally")
1	
2	
3	
4	
5	
6	

4. ARE YOU A 100% LISTENER?
(Testing your listening skills)

Are you a 100% listener? This chapter is your opportunity to test your listening ability. Understanding where we are today with our listening skills starts the process of improving.

An important first step in growing our listening skills is recognizing that everyone listens in different ways and listens for different things. Everyone has a unique combination of three important factors that affect our listening:

- The sources of information we use in our own listening process;

- Our specific listening skills;

- How we listen and the filters we naturally apply when we listen.

The first two components are covered in this chapter. How we listen and the filters we naturally apply are covered in the next chapter.

Sources of information in listening

When we listen, we take in information ("catch the communication pass") and take meaning from both verbal and non-verbal communication. There are three principal sources of information:

- Specific words and the speaker's word choice;

- Tone of voice and inflection;

- Body language.

Tone of voice, inflection, and the body language are all part of non-verbal communication and are associated with the autonomic nervous system – we do it automatically, without thinking about it. If we are thinking or feeling something, our body responds naturally with these non-verbal communications. They can be controlled (i.e., a poker face or predetermined and controlled tone of voice), but generally are an involuntary reflection of what we are thinking or feeling at the moment we are speaking. Actors work from a script and have predetermined word choice. They create award-winning characters by directing or controlling their non-verbal communications, especially body language.

- **Tone of voice** – relates to the energy and mood behind the message (i.e., tired, bored, disinterested, happy, excited, enthusiastic, angry, etc.).

- **Inflection** – relates to the emphasis on specific words. Where the speaker places emphasis indicates which words are most important in understanding the meaning. Example: *I* am happy to see you vs. I am *happy* to see you vs. I am happy to *see* you vs. I am happy to see *you*.

- **Body language** – physically reveals what you are feeling or thinking. If you don't think body language is a natural extension of your feelings or thoughts, then watch yourself next time you talk on the phone. Take note of how your facial expression changes or observe your large and small arm or hand movements as you talk. The person you are talking to cannot see you, so why is your body talking?

Many people make the assumption that all people listen the same way – "the way I do". It simply is not true. Some people take most of their message from the words, while others rely more on tone of voice or inflection. Others take most of their information from body language. How we listen frequently is impacted by our state of mind – whether we are relaxed or in a stressful situation.

What are *your* sources of information? How important is each to you? The answers will help you understand better how you listen and where you are more effective as a listener. It will help you understand how different methods of communication affect your ability to fully understand – face-to-face, telephone, email, etc. There are no right or wrong answers – only differences in how we receive information.

Now let's quantify your sources of information when listening (in a qualitative kind of way). Think about how you listen and the importance of each of the three sources of information under two different circumstances – comfort and stress. Estimate the percentage of information that comes from each source (1) when things are going well, and (2) when you are facing barriers, are blocked, frustrated, or under stress. Work all three areas first from your comfort zone. Then do all three again, but this time from your stress zone. The individual percentages should add to 100% in each column. In considering how important body language is to you, try blocking your view of the other person's face when you are having a conversation. What have you lost?

SOURCES OF INFORMATION IN LISTENING
(How I get information and meaning)

SOURCE OF INFORMATION	In My Comfort Zone	In My Stress Zone
Words – word choice	%	%
Tone of voice / inflection	%	%
Body language	%	%
Totals	100%	100%

Listening skills inventory

Now that you have quantified the importance of the different sources of information, let's inventory your specific listening skills. Please rate yourself on a scale of 1 to 10 (10 = highest) in each of the 10 areas in the skills inventory on pages 16 and 17. First, answer all questions from your comfort zone. Then do them again from your stress zone. Total all of the numbers at the bottom of page 17. The individual percentages will tell you how close you are to a 100% listener. Be honest with yourself. This is not an ego trip. The purpose of this inventory is to measure your current skills and identify areas where you can grow.

What did you learn about yourself?

We all are different. We depend on different combinations of information sources when listening. One of the authors depends on non-verbal input for 80% of her listening input, with 60% coming from body language while the other gets only about 20% from body language when in his comfort zone. We all have developed our listening skills to a greater or lesser degree. Understanding where we are strong and weak and how our listening changes under stress or in conflict will help us be more effective in relationships, managing, leading, and every other part of our lives.

Now pause and take a few minutes to think about your results from these two inventories. Think about what you learned about yourself as a listener, and about listening in general. What are the implications for you personally? Record your conclusions in the table on page 18. The following questions may stimulate your thinking.

- Where are you most in need of improvement in the 10 areas of listening?

- Do you tend to listen for specific word choice or for general meaning and concepts? What are the implications for you in communicating?

- How important is reading body language to your listening? What does that mean in terms of how you communicate and the effectiveness of your listening in different communication methods – face-to-face, telephone, and email?

- What happens to your listening skills in conflict or stress? Many people lose listening skills when under stress. What are the implications for you?

- Non-verbal communication (yours and the other person's) is an important part of the listening process. It is part of your rating in questions 2, 4, 5, and 10. What are the implications of what you are doing with your body (questions 4 and 10) to your effectiveness as a listener?

ARE YOU A 100% LISTENER?

Please rate yourself on a scale of 1 to 10 (10 = highest) in each of the 10 areas under two conditions: (1) when things are going well and you are not blocked, frustrated, or under stress, and (2) when you are facing barriers, are blocked, or under stress. Answer all 10 questions first from your comfort zone. Then return and do them again from your stress zone. Total the numbers at the bottom of page 17. The individual percentages will tell you how close you are to being a 100% listener.

	QUESTIONS	In Comfort Zone	In Stress Zone
1	How much do you pay attention to specific word choices and nuances when you are listening (vs. just listening for general meaning)?		
2	How much do you pay attention to the other person's tone of voice or inflection when listening?		
3	How often do you wait for the other person to finish talking completely before you start talking? At the highest level (10), there actually might be a slight pause in the conversation before you start to talk.		
4	How well do you maintain eye or face contact (the ability to watch the other person's facial reaction) when you are talking?		
5	How well do you understand *and* read body language?		
6	How much do you listen to understand fully what the other person is saying (vs. listening only partially and thinking of what you will say or how you will respond when the other person stops talking)?		

7	How often do you paraphrase what the other person says or ask a question to ensure your understanding before continuing the conversation, particularly for more difficult ideas or when someone is upset or angry?		
8	How often do you put yourself in other people's shoes, listening empathetically to understand how they feel or where they are coming from (i.e., emotionally, logically, or experientially)?		
9	How much do you listen for different meanings or messages based on cultural, regional, or gender differences?		
10	How well do you communicate your interest in listening (i.e., your body language or verbal acknowledgment of what the other person is saying)?		
	TOTAL	%	%

How did you rate yourself?

90 to 100% – Either outstanding or who are you kidding?;
80 to 90% – Very good listener; **70 to 80%** – Good listener;
60 to 70% – Average listener; **50 to 60%** – Fair listener, need work;
40 to 50% – Poor listener, really need work;
Less than 40% – What did they say?

WHAT I LEARNED ABOUT MYSELF AND LISTENING IN GENERAL

1	
2	
3	
4	
5	
6	

5. WE DON'T HEAR WHAT WE FILTER OUT
(Our innate listening problems and filters)

Have you noticed that some people appear to listen for just enough detail to get into action or start solving a problem and then stop listening, even though the conversation continues on? They seem to filter out or ignore information on the feelings of others or a lot of the detail that people give them.

Other people are intent on listening for detail and logic, but shy away from lots of conversation about people, the company picnic, pets, and other personal details. When they do have to participate in these conversations, you just know that the words are going in, but not staying.

Others seem to be intuitive listeners. They intuitively know where people are coming from and how to be helpful with a minimum of verbal input. But don't expect them to remember all of the details or exactly what was said. They can give you the concept and paraphrase a conversation, but are hard pressed to recall specific words.

In the communication process, we are physically part of the conversation. We are listening, but we just don't seem to hear some things. In truth, we are filtering those things out, often unconsciously. Why? It is naturally part of who we are and, at the same time, tied to what makes us successful at what we do.

Does that seem like a contradiction? It is not. But it does mean that we all have our own set of innate listening problems and filters. We are born with them. They are part of us, but they can be overcome if we understand what motivates us and work at changing the "less natural" listening behaviors. These problems are tied directly to what motivates us and builds our self-worth and our sense of self-esteem. Therefore, an important step in improving as listeners is to recognize who we are and what natural, innate problems and filters we carry around with us.

We need to dip into motivational theory here, but will keep it simple and practical. Please bear with us. What you learn will help you overcome some of your listening problems, and may give you a better understanding of yourself and other people.

Dr. Elias H. Porter (1914 - 1987) developed an excellent explanation for how we behave and what motivates us as individuals – Relationship Awareness Theory[1]. The following concepts are at the heart of his theory.

- We are born with circuitry in our brain that defines our perceptions. (Some believe that these perceptions can be affected by major life experiences.)

- These perceptions determine what we value and what motivates us.

- We are all a unique blend of three motivational factors (described in the following paragraph).

- What we value determines what makes us feel good about ourselves.

- We do what we do to feel good about ourselves.

- Therefore, whenever possible, our behavior and how we interact with others or respond to situations is a reflection of what motivates us and how we choose to act in order to reinforce our sense of well being.

- We have two sets of perceptions/values – one when things are going well, and another when we are under stress or in conflict. Therefore, what we value, what motivates us, and how we behave changes as we move from comfort to stress. (We all have a little Dr. Jekyl and Mr. Hyde in us.) Some people's values and behavior change pretty dramatically as they move from comfort to stress, and others hardly at all.

[1] Relationship Awareness Theory is copyrighted by Personal Strengths Publishing. For more information on Relationship Awareness Theory, contact Personal Strengths Publishing at personalstrengths.com.

- Weaknesses are no more or no less than our strengths overdone or misapplied. In other words, we do not have weaknesses that have to be fixed. Instead, we have strengths that need to be controlled and better applied. For example, trust overdone becomes gullibility. Confidence overdone becomes arrogance. Flexibility overdone becomes wishy-washy.

Three basic motivational factors or motivational drives are uniquely combined in each of us. Some of us tend to be driven primarily by one of these motivational values while others are fairly complex blends of two or more of these three motivational values. There is no right or wrong grouping of motivational values. Every combination brings its own unique set of strengths and weaknesses. These motivational drives are:

- The desire to be in action and complete a task;

- The desire to nurture and help or support others; and

- The desire to be self-reliant, logically structured, and self-contained.

What's the point? How does all of this theory tie back to improving our listening abilities? Our perceptions and values create filters and innate listening patterns in *what* we listen for and *how* we listen. Each of these listening patterns has strengths that support our motivational values and translate into natural weaknesses in our listening. For example, some people naturally listen for just enough detail to get into action. Some listen for information that tells them how people feel in order to be helpful to others. Some listen for detail and logic. Some listen for information that relates to being part of a group and building consensus.

The following table includes examples from our research and training. As you read the table, think about what motivates you and how you listen. Hopefully, you will identify more strongly with one group of motivational values and listening patterns. Please remember the following points when considering the examples in the table.

- First, all generalizations are wrong (with the possible exception of this generalization).

- Second, these examples are simplified illustrations of listening characteristics and problems for people with distinctly different motivational values.

- Third, since we are a unique blend of the three motivational values, many of us have listening behavior or filters that are a blend of several different motivational values.

The important point is to recognize that we all have innate listening filters and natural behavior that is tied to what enhances our sense of self-worth. We are likely to feel better about ourselves when we apply our natural filters and behavior.

We are who we are. Developing better listening skills does not require us to change who we are. It only requires that we (1) change how we think about listening, (2) understand the differences we all have in our natural filters and behavior, and (3) recognize what we are missing with our natural listening behavior. If we can recognize and manage these innate characteristics, we will hear and understand more and have more successful interpersonal interactions.

TYPICAL LISTENING PATTERNS BY WHAT MOTIVATES US

The following listening patterns are representative of how people with different motivational values naturally listen. Listening problems can be overcome by applying one or more of the 10 listening tools included in this book.

PEOPLE MOTIVATED BY GETTING INTO IMMEDIATE ACTION AND COMPLETING THE TASK
How they listen:
<ul><li>Impatiently – "Get to the point!"</li><li>Well, but only for a short period of time (often well before the communication ends)</li></ul>
Listening filters:
<ul><li>Listen for information needed to get into action – goals, action plans, costs, benefits, etc.</li><li>Listen for big picture and barriers to action</li><li>Tend to filter out "unnecessary" data and details</li><li>Tend to filter out "unnecessary" information about how people feel</li></ul>
Typical listening problems:
<ul><li>Generalist listener</li><li>Incomplete information about details and feelings of others</li><li>Often insensitive to the subtleties of body language</li><li>Start processing ideas on how to get into action while trying to listen</li></ul>

PEOPLE MOTIVATED BY NURTURING AND HELPING OTHERS

How they listen:

- Empathetically and intuitively
- Tend to place heavy emphasis on non-verbal messages, especially body language – they watch as much as listen

Listening filters:

- Listen for information to be more helpful to others – pain, distress, joy, conflict, etc.
- Listen for motive, intent, and hidden agendas
- Listen for general ideas and concepts, not detail
- Tend to filter out "unnecessary" details

Typical listening problems:

- Generalist listener – see big picture, but may miss important details
- Overly sensitive to non-verbal communication – whether it is intended or unintended
- Distracted from details of discussion by emotional state of the speaker
- Negative listening response to perceived negative people, anger, rudeness, or sarcasm
- Start processing ideas on how to be helpful while trying to listen

PEOPLE MOTIVATED BY BEING SELF-CONTAINED, LOGICAL, AND RIGHT

How they listen:

- Logically and unemotionally
- Quantitatively
- Tend to place heavy emphasis on words and details

Listening filters:

- Listen for details or information to apply analysis and logic – facts, logic, process
- Listen for clues to validate speaker as a credible source of information
- Tend to filter out emotional content (feelings of others) as "unnecessary"
- Tend to consider time factors less important than "getting it right"

Typical listening problems:

- Specifist listener - may miss some of the big picture
- Often insensitive to body language and subtle non-verbal communication
- Negative listening response to perception that they are wrong
- Start solving problems while trying to listen
- Sometimes, a delayed understanding of their own feelings

PEOPLE MOTIVATED BY BEING FLEXIBLE, PART OF THE GROUP, AND BUILDING CONSENSUS

How they listen:

- Inconsistently
- Sometimes for a very long time
- Tend to place heavy emphasis on word *choice*

Listening filters:

- Listen to understand the situation
- Listen for different perspectives and opinions - to get all points of view
- Listen for agreement and exceptions, in order to build consensus

Typical listening problems:

- Don't filter enough - get information overload that can lead to confusion or indecision
- People who are rigid, adamant, or have unyielding attitudes - resistive to consensus building
- Connecting with people who have extreme motivational values - too quick to get into action, too deeply into feelings and emotions of others, too analytical and self-contained
- Start thinking about how to integrate ideas while trying to listen
- Often interrupt other person to extend or expand an idea

You may be asking yourself, "How can I use this information to be a better listener?" The answer is simple. It helps us understand where we are likely to be incomplete or ineffective listeners – what we naturally filter out and how we need to change our mindset and our listening behavior in order to be more effective listeners. Recognizing who we are helps us rethink how we can interact with other people to facilitate a conversation that better fits with our natural listening style while not demotivating the other person.

Let's consider several examples:

- **A person motivated by getting into action and getting the task completed**: This person is likely to listen impatiently and often filters out information on the feelings of others and "unnecessary" details. "Too much" conversation is considered a barrier to action. If you have this kind of motivational value, you should consider changing your mindset to *redefine the task* to include listening for how others are affected or feel and listening a little more to the details. Yes, it might slightly delay getting into action, but this mindset can produce results faster, and results that are more likely to succeed the first time around. You also can ask someone to "get to the point" more politely or ask that people give you the bottom line first and then give you the details.

- **A person motivated by nurturing and helping others**: This person can be distracted from the conversation by the non-verbal input that he or she gets intuitively. Non-verbal communication is a very powerful tool. It is great to know how people feel and whether they can be trusted, but it also is useful to know the time, cost, date, who is involved, and other specific details important to the speaker. If you have these motivational values and listening tendencies, then you should find a way to get more of the details out of respect for the speaker and to be in a better position to help. For example, a note pad is useful so that you can capture the details for later reference. As one person who is motivated by nurturing and helping others said about details, "The details just kind of blow by me. The only details that really bother me are the ones <u>you</u> ask for and I can't produce, because then I have failed to help you."

- **A person motivated by being self-contained, logical, and right**: This person is likely to filter out information on the feelings of others and "unnecessary" emotional content. There is a tendency to filter out time and budget demands that get in the way of "getting the right answer." If you have these motivational values, consider changing your mindset to include people considerations in the getting to the "right" solution and the importance of balancing timeliness with the "right" solution. True success is being right <u>on time</u>. You also should find ways to take the sting out of communication that implies (or makes you infer) that you are wrong.

- **A person motivated by being flexible, part of the group, and building consensus** (getting people to agree): This person can listen *too* long to *too* many people and take *too* long to get people to agree before making a decision. The problem may be not enough filtering. If you have these motivational values, consider changing your mind set to balance the need for input with the need to make a decision and move ahead.

Now take a few minutes. Think about this information and what motivates you. Then ask yourself the following kinds of questions.

- How do I listen?

- What do I listen for?

- What kinds of listening problems do I have that relate to my motivational values?

- How do these innate listening characteristics impact my effectiveness as a listener?

- What does this tell me about my listening?

Then think about the benefits of better managing your natural listening filters and characteristics. Record your thoughts in the following table.

	MY INNATE LISTENING ISSUES	
	Listening characteristics or filters	Benefits to me for better managing
1		
2		
3		
4		
5		

6. WORDS MEAN DIFFERENT THINGS TO DIFFERENT PEOPLE
(How our perceptions and motivational values affect the meaning of words)

"There we were, having a nice conversation. Suddenly it was like we were speaking two different languages. I said this and he heard that. I just don't understand why we have so much trouble communicating." Sound familiar? There is a logical explanation.

We actually are speaking different languages even though we are both using English. Winston Churchill said of Americans and the British, "We are two peoples divided by a common language." He was referring to cultural differences between two English speaking countries. However, the same principle applies to people with different motivational values.

Some people respond with, "What? All you have to do is know what the word means. If you don't, just get out a dictionary." Yes. There is a dictionary, but it is only a starting place. We each have our own heart level definitions for many words, and those definitions change between people with different motivational values.

We routinely get excellent illustrations of this point from our communications training. We break the class into groups with similar motivational values. We give them the same words to define *as a group*. Their job is to come up with sentence or phrase definitions that they all agree on. Here is one example of the differences in meaning by motivational values.

"Happiness":

- "A never ending stream of challenges." – *people motivated by getting into action and task completion*

- "Being in an warm, harmonious environment that respects the feelings of others and is filled with helpful, caring people, in which everyone achieves their full potential." – *people motivated by being nurturing and helpful*

- "Being right, *and* having public affirmation that we are right." – *people motivated by being self-reliant and logical*

- "Keeping all parts of our life in balance and in harmony: work, career, family, and our social life." – *people motivated by being flexible, part of the group, and building consensus*

Imagine the potential misunderstanding, stress, or conflict when people with one set of motivational values say to another, "You are going to love this new job. It will cover you with happiness."
"Help" vs. "appreciate":

The two authors have different motivational values, and these differences affect their word choice in something so simple as asking the other to do something.

- Laura makes a request for assistance by saying, "It would be a big help if you would …."

- Olin makes the same request by saying, " I would appreciate it if you would …."

- Both requests have the same sense of urgency in the mind of the speaker. However, to Laura *"help"* means, "I will do it right now because it's important" and *"appreciate"* means "I'll put it on my mental 'to do' list and get to it eventually."

- To Olin, *"help"* might have a sting in some circumstances and raise a strong-willed reaction along the lines of "What? Are you implying that I don't help out around here?"

The differences in word meaning are remarkable. As one person said, "We have 60,000 words, but 600,000 meanings." It's a wonder we communicate at all. The words we hear pass through our perceptual filters and change in meaning. Unfortunately, we tend to think that other people are like us in their communication and that a word means the same thing to them as it does to us.

Now you try it. Select a few words and define them. Then get several other people to come up with their definitions. Here are a few suggestions to get you started: success, failure, leadership.

One of the keys to being a 100% listener is understanding the motivational values of the person talking to you. This is part of putting yourself in the other person's shoes and being an empathetic listener (see Chapter 15 for more on the tool of Empathetic Listening). Chapter 19 expands this principle – words mean different things to different people – and deals with the listening tool of using a Translator to get to the true meaning and take the sting out of words.

7. OK. SO HOW DO I BECOME A 100% LISTENER?
(Starting on the path of self-improvement)

As with any improvement process, there are three tests to determine how successful we will be. First, we need to know where we are and identify areas that need improvement. Second, we need to admit that improvement is needed in specific areas. Third, we need to understand how the improvement will be personally beneficial – it needs to matter to us personally.

If you have been doing the exercises as you read the chapters, you already have completed the first test for successful improvement. You should have a pretty good idea of:

- Your sources of listening information and how they change when you move from comfort to stress (page 13);

- How close you are to a 100% listener in the 10 key areas of listening from your listening skills inventory (pages 16 and 17);

- Your innate or natural listening filters and an idea of how you listen – things that are tied to your own motivational values.

How did you do? What did you learn about yourself and your listening skills? Do you think that an improvement is needed? If you answered yes, you just passed the second test. You have recognized the need and will get value from the rest of this book. If your answer is "no", please go find a nice novel to read and give this book to someone else.

The third test for successful improvement centers around two questions. Why is it important for me to improve my listening skills? How will I benefit personally? If you have not answered that question yet, take a few minutes. Think about how your interactions at work, at home, and in other relationships will benefit from becoming a better listener. You may want to review the benefits in Chapter 3. Write down four or five (or more) personal benefits. As part of your thinking, review what you wrote on page 10 and add to it as appropriate. You just passed the third test for success!

Now you truly are ready to maximize your listening skills, overcome your innate listening problems, and start down the road to becoming a 100% listener. You also are on your way to improving your emotional intelligence by understanding yourself and others better.

The remaining chapters give you a set of 10 listening tools. We recommend reading all of the chapters. Then go back to review the chapters addressing those areas that you have identified for personal improvement. The last chapter is for your personal action plan. We recommend periodic retesting to measure how you are doing on the road to 100% listening. Pages 96 through 99 include a place to retest your listening skills and record progress and improvement over time.

8. HELLO? IS ANYONE HOME?
(*Tool #1 – Being Fully Present*)

You are having a conversation with someone. It may be in an office, at a party, in a business meeting, or on the phone. Maybe they are multi-tasking at their desk. They might be looking at someone across the room at a party. In a meeting, they could be doodling, looking at something not related to the meeting, or engaged in a running side conversation. On the phone you may hear the clicking of computer keys in the background. These people are not focused on you and what you are saying. How do *you* feel when they are not fully present when you are talking?

A husband is partially watching a ball game on TV and glancing at the newspaper while his wife is talking. Finally, in frustration, she says, "You're not listening to me!" He responds, "Yes I am." and repeats back what she said with surprising accuracy. She pauses and then announces, "Well, you may have heard me, but you're still not listening." What is the problem here? Really listening is more than just getting the information; it also is being fully present for the speaker. Being fully present is all about respect.

We create real problems for ourselves when we are not completely involved as listeners. An example from an executive makes the point for the office setting:

> "It was a busy day and one of my staff dropped in to talk about a problem. I listened for a few minutes, understood what the problem was, and then started to review some of my e-mail and listened as he went on and on and on about the details of it all. I politely acknowledged what he was saying with an 'Un-huh' at the appropriate times. At the end of the conversation, I had the sense that he went away frustrated and unsatisfied. It also occurred to me that he might have gotten to the point and stopped repeating himself if I had given him my full attention. If so, it would have saved me 15 to 20 minutes to do other things with my time."

Why is it so important to be fully present when listening? What are the benefits to us personally? People want to be heard. They want to be respected as a person. Being fully present is the one single thing that makes most interpersonal interactions easier, more productive, and more pleasant. People are more motivated, feel better about themselves, are more comfortable with the outcome of the conversation, and are more likely to look forward to the next conversation. In conflict situations, people are more likely to believe that their opinion was heard and considered, even if the decision favored a different viewpoint. It can make the difference between reluctant acceptance and ongoing conflict.

Some people refer to this tool as "putting on big ears." We believe that it is more than appearance. It is more than just "big ears." It is full engagement with your mind and your body.

The power of Being Fully Present should not be underestimated. Politicians use this tool to gain votes and loyalty. When we hear someone describe a politician by saying "He made me feel like I was the only one in the room!" we know that the politician has mastered the tool of Being Fully Present. It is exhilarating and flattering when someone makes us feel important and respected by giving us his or her full attention.

Too many people think of listening as an activity, which explains why multi-tasking is okay. In fact, listening is a process. This change in mindset is the first step in applying the tool of being fully present.

Are you having trouble being fully present? Here are a few ideas that we have picked up that may help.

- Put the concept of being fully present in terms of respect. Every human being is deserving of respect. This is a personal mindset issue. It especially applies when we do not respect the person or his/her ideas for whatever reason.

- How do I deal with a person who goes on and on and on and on? "How much of this fully present thing do I have to do anyway?" Being fully present does not mean that you have to listen to everything that a person may want to say. It means that you should be fully present to the conversation that you have, but you do have some control over the direction and length of the conversation. If people seem to want to go on and on, combine the tool of Being Fully Present with the art of the skillful redirect (more on this in the next chapter).

- Keep in mind that people who believe that they are being heard and respected typically get to the point faster and feel less of a need to repeat things or go into more and more detail. They know that you got the point the first time and do not need the unabridged edition. They will be more willing to accept the skillful redirect or an end to the conversation without feeling brushed off or dismissed.

*   *   *   *   *

The tool of Being Fully Present is a foundational tool for becoming a 100% listener. It always should be in use and should be used in combination with the other nine tools.

9. PARDON ME WHILE I STEP ON YOUR WORDS
(*Tool # 2 - Controlled Verbal And Mental Response* – Part 1)

Most of us are guilty of interrupting others before they have finished speaking. When we think about it or have to defend ourselves, there always is a good reason:

"Just get to the point! If you can't, I will."

"I'm really just trying to help them complete their thought."

"It's how I show that I really understand."

"The idea was great; I was only adding my thinking to it,
and maybe building on it."

"I'm right. They're wrong, and I will prove it to them."

"That was a really stupid idea. We needed to get
back on track."

"My ideas are more important (or better) than theirs."

"I'm more important than they are, so they should be
listening to me."

"Ho hum! *Bo-o-oring*! Anything to change the subject."

"I'm the boss, and I just want to tell them what to do."

"I am (or want to be) the center of this discussion."

Do any of these excuses sound familiar? We are incomplete listeners, and this causes us to interrupt the speaker with our words. We do this for many reasons. Some of the reasons are negative or self-serving – ego, rudeness, lack of respect, anger, or not wanting to take the time to listen completely.

Other reasons are more altruistic – helping the speaker complete a difficult idea or showing empathy. Sometimes our motive is based on the desire to build consensus or add value to the speaker's ideas in a positive way. And sometimes we get so excited or enthusiastic that we just can't help ourselves.

This tendency or habit of stepping on other peoples' words can add value by shortening the conversation or bringing ideas into sharper focus for us, but at a real cost. Cutting people off (the less polite way of saying that we are stepping on their words) has serious negatives *for us as listeners*.

The downside far outweighs whatever positive we can rationalize. We may have an incomplete or incorrect understanding because we did not get the full content of the idea being presented. Lacking the complete idea, we can go off and make an incorrect decision. Lacking a complete understanding of the idea or speaker's intent, we can respond in a way that creates stress in the speaker or conflict between us.
In extreme cases, this practice can demotivate the speaker or trigger a strong-willed reaction. We are demonstrating that we really are not interested in listening completely. The result? The speaker may lose interest in correcting your misunderstanding or continuing to be part of the discussion. Why? Because it can be interpreted correctly as a lack of respect. Who loses? We lose or, in some cases, we both lose because we limit our information and understanding. We also may turn a conversation into a more negative exchange or drive a situation into deeper conflict.

Our tendency to step on the speaker's words shows that we are not listening completely. When we are experiencing strong emotions (such as impatience, disagreement, anger, or lack of respect), our body language not only reinforces the sense that we are not listening, but can intensify the reaction of the speaker.

Now take a minute. Think about four or five situations where you cut off the speaker. What was your thinking – the rationale that made it "OK" in your mind? What kinds of problems did you create with bosses, co-workers, subordinates, friends, or family members? Now think about the positive benefits *to you* of letting people complete their thoughts. Remember, it needs to matter personally if you are going to be successful in changing your behavior. Otherwise, the improvement is just a good idea that has no roots.

Here are a few suggestions that will help you break this habit and become less likely to interrupt people. Consider the types of situations that are most difficult for you as a listener, and add other ideas that will help you curb this habit.

- Think of this tool as mentally biting your tongue, or physically biting your tongue if you must.

- Remember that your body may be talking even if you have controlled your tongue. Try to put your body in a listening posture to help control this habit (more on this in Chapter 18).

- Consider apologizing when you catch yourself interrupting people. It is a little humbling and a very personal reminder to listen more completely.

- Think of the speaker as deserving respect as a human being, even if you do not respect or agree with the ideas or ways of expressing them.

- Remember that some people, particularly analytical people, need to take time to put things into a logical flow – building up from the data or detail to the conclusion and recommendation. The value comes in listening completely.

- Practice the art of the skillful redirect (see pages 41 and 42). This is an excellent tool for those of us who want the speaker to get to the point quickly.

- Remember that many people go on at length to ensure a complete understanding because they think that you are not listening, evidenced by our cutting off their words, possibly reinforced by our body language. Letting people finish their thoughts may actually shorten the conversation, especially if combined with a skillful redirect and the tool of Being Fully Present.

- Let there be a slight pause in the conversation between the speaker finishing and your response. Try using this approach if you are having real difficulty breaking this bad listening habit. The slight pause is a very effective tool in conflict or when dealing with emotional situations. It gives the speaker a sense that you are listening completely and empathetically, and then reflecting on what was said before responding. It also gives you time to respond in a way that helps defuse a difficult situation rather than fueling it.

- Consider your strong will and ego. Are they getting in the way of being a 100% listener in this area? These are personal issues that all of us need to address from our own perspective.

The art of the skillful redirect

The art of the skillful redirect is an excellent tool to help you politely get people to the point quickly or to shorten conversations that seem to go on and on. Using this tool shows emotional intelligence in your interaction with others. Here are several examples to illustrate proper use of the skillful redirect. Think about your personal interactions and adapt this tool to your own style.

- "You have some really good ideas here. Could you give me the bottom line first, and then we can talk about the details."

- "You have some good ideas here. Come; walk with me while I get to my next meeting (or the car or the board room, etc.)" This artful redirect adds value because it physically removes the individual from your office.

- "You have some good ideas here. Unfortunately, I don't have time right now to hear them in detail. Could we set up a time later or over lunch, etc. to talk about them more?"

*   *   *   *   *

The tool of the Controlled Verbal And Mental Response is a powerful tool. It is a valuable part of being fully present. It shows respect, gives us the opportunity to be more thoughtful in our response, and actually may give us valuable information that would have been cut off. While it may seem to add interminable delays during the conversation at an emotional level, it really adds little actual time and actually may shorten the total time in a conversation, especially if your interruptions cause the speaker to want to elaborate with more information because it is evident that you are not listening.

10. I'M READY FOR YOU JUST AS SOON AS YOU STOP TALKING!
(*Tool #2 – Controlled Verbal And Mental Response* – Part 2)

We're getting better at listening when we have learned to control our verbal interruptions. We don't step on the other person's words as much now that we are using the tool of the Controlled Verbal Response, but many of us are still shutting down our listening to start thinking about how we will respond or what we will do with the partial information that we did hear.

"Wait a minute. Are you telling me to stop thinking and not even begin to formulate a response until after the other guy stops talking? I'd look like a moron." No. That is not what this tool is all about. It is about controlling our mental response to be more effective in what we are hearing. We naturally process information as we receive it. The human mind generally processes information faster than we can take it in so that we can respond as the other person completes his or her thought.

The listening problem comes when we *shut down* our listening and focus primarily on our own thoughts. Think of it as two voices – an outside voice (the other person talking) and our own inner voice. If we are talking to ourselves instead of listening, the inner voice often overpowers the outside voice – what the other person is saying. For example, what happens to our listening when we are rehearsing what we will say when the other person pauses long enough for us to get our words in?

Shutting down our listening is a common problem, but people with different motivational values do it for different reasons. Three examples:

- If we tell analytical people that they are wrong without providing the proper, logically presented supporting information, then they often will stop listening and internally begin the process of proving that they are right and you are wrong, even if the thoughts are never verbalized.

- We can give people motivated by being in action and task completion more information than they need to get into action. These action-oriented people often stop listening early in the conversation and begin planning what they will do to get going.

- We communicate to people who are motivated by helping and nurturing others that they have failed at some task. When they perceive criticism, these people often stop listening and begin chastising themselves for failing to be helpful. The negative message may be delivered intentionally or unintentionally through words or non-verbal communication.

The habit of thinking to ourselves instead of listening to others is similar to cutting people off, but it is much more subtle. When we cut a person off, our listening behavior is easy to see. The speaker knows that we have stopped listening or have an incomplete understanding. When we stop listening, we may still appear to be taking it in, but little is being received. We do this for many reasons beyond the three examples tied to motivational values:

- When we are in a debate or heated discussion, we frequently are more focused on making our point than we are interested in hearing the other person's ideas or fully understanding them.

- Sometimes we see a conversation as more of a communication from us to others. We are more interested in telling people than we are in listening to what others think or feel.

- We might be nervous or uncertain and are thinking about what to say or how to say it.

- We want to look good in the conversation. We are focused more on ourselves than the other person.

- Some of us are guilty of believing that our words or ideas are more important than the other person's.

- We are trying to terminate a conversation, but are being more polite about it than simply cutting the other person off.

Whatever the cause, our inner voice overpowers the outside voice. We are interrupting our own listening process to think about how we will respond or what we will do when they stop talking. Listening to our inner voice is the real core problem for both listening incompletely while we think of a response and actually going to the next step and cutting people off with our words.

Now think about your own listening. Where or when do you shut down your listening? How can you better manage your loss of mental control? What else can you do to deal with these lapses?

Here are a few suggestions that we have picked up to help you attack this listening problem, use this tool of Controlled Verbal And Mental Response, and remain fully present.

- Remember that, at its root, this is a mental control or emotional intelligence issue, and that *you* are in control of whether you remain fully present in a conversation or presentation. Tell your inner voice to be quiet. Discipline yourself not to be distracted by other thoughts.

- As with stepping on the other person's words, make the emotional intelligence commitment to think of the other person as deserving of your respect as a human being. This will help you to focus on your listening and tune out your inner voice.

- When you catch yourself shutting down your listening, be honest and apologize. Ask the speaker to repeat what you missed. "I'm sorry. I missed that last point. Would you please repeat it?" It is a little humbling and will help remind you to stay engaged mentally. This is an admission that you were not fully present, but it also demonstrates that you really do want the input.

- Remember that all human beings have a tendency to be distracted by internal and external things. This will make your apology and request for a repeat a little easier to make.

- Consider analyzing why your inner voice won out over the outside voice. After the conversation, replay in your mind what you were doing or thinking during the conversation. What triggered the dominance of your inner voice? This may help you catch yourself in the future.

- Applying the tool of Being Fully Present and positioning your body to be in more of a receive posture will help (more on using your body language in Chapters 17 and 18).

- Finding ways to take the critical sting out of what was said ("They may have said that, but they didn't really mean it as personal criticism") can help you keep your reception channels open. Try applying the tool of Using A Translator to take the sting out of words (Chapter 19).

*   *   *   *   *

Applying the tool of Controlled Verbal And Mental Response is an integral part of being fully present. Controlling what we do with our mouth and our mind as we listen improves what we receive as well as what we communicate to the speaker.

11. LISTEN TO THE WORDS – THEY HAVE SPECIAL MEANING
(*Tool #3 – Listening Specifically To Word Choice*)

Listening to the specific words comes more easily to some than others. The two authors represent both ends of the spectrum in the area of listening specifically to word choice – one is a specifist in listening and the other is very much a generalist.

Some years ago, Laura – our generalist listener – wanted to sound 'with it' in a conversation with one of our teenage daughters. She asked the question, "Are you going to see that new movie, 'Cast Iron Vest'?" The teen responded with a perplexed look, "You mean 'Full Metal Jacket'?" The concept was there – heavy metal clothing – but generalized. Generalist thinkers typically listen for the concept as opposed to the specific details or word choice.

Are you a specifist or generalist when listening? This is an important consideration for us as listeners. The words are important, and many people carefully choose specific words to convey subtleties of meaning.

Some of us pay close attention to the words themselves. These people can repeat exactly what was said or at least a very close approximation, capturing specific words. For these people, words convey detailed meaning. Choosing one word instead of another conveys shades of meaning. For these people, the specific fact or idea is important. For example, specific word choice provides a logical basis for a thesis or the subtleties of meaning in a report. The choice of words also may show shades of acceptance of an idea that help the listener identify points of difference and be more effective in building consensus. Some words are particularly motivating or demotivating to people with different motivational values. On the negative side, people who rate themselves highly in listening for specific word choice may be less effective in listening for the big picture.

For other people, words are just a general vehicle to convey a concept or idea. They tend to generalize words when listening. The specific word is heard, but is translated or generalized during the hearing process. It is remembered, but more as an idea or concept rather than as a specific set of words. As one generalized listener said,

> *"I'm listening for where you're coming from and what you mean beyond what you are saying. I want to capture your idea and make it my own. Isn't that the height of listening and respect to the speaker – to take it in and make it my own? I'm not oblivious to details. I take in the occasional word, but why clutter up my mind with the specific word choice when I can go to some source and get the details if I need them later. If I focus on the details, I'll miss the concept."*

Giving people who generalize when listening the responsibility for taking flip chart notes can be both amusing and frustrating at the same time. The words recorded on paper capture the idea, but may bear little resemblance to the actual words used in the discussion.

Generalized listeners can bring special strengths – the ability to capture an idea in a way that encourages open-ended or out-of-the-box thinking. Many people who are generalized listeners are excellent strategic thinkers. The obvious weakness is that the preciseness of the communication is lost in the listening process. The results can include (1) giving the impression that we are not listening carefully; (2) contributing to confusion in negotiation or other communications; and (3) having a more limited ability to pass on detailed instructions that require some specificity.

Even though words have defined meanings, sometimes all of us are guilty of changing the meaning as the word passes through our own perceptual filters, as described in Chapter 6.

How can generalized listeners become more effective at hearing the details? Here are a few tips that we have picked up. Add to this list based on your own experience and what you know about yourself.

- Try taking notes to capture important words and details to review later if the details are needed. This approach leaves your mind free to process and capture the broader concept.

- As a point of emotional intelligence, be more aware that you are not getting the details. Remember that generalizing what you heard can create problems and miscommunication with some people.

- Remember that precise definition is important to many people and that they take care to choose their words to communicate their meaning. Being more effective in picking up key words can confirm that you are listening and showing respect for these people.

- Try using your inner voice to capture specific details that are important, but without overpowering the outside voice of the speaker – when in conflict, when negotiating details of an agreement, when getting information to pass on to someone else, and so on. Repeat the words to yourself as a way to secure the specific words.

- If the details are important and you depend heavily on body language for your listening, sometimes the body language messages from the other person interfere with hearing the specific words. Try looking less directly at the person as you listen in order to reduce the distraction from the body language messages. However, make sure that the rest of your own body language demonstrates that you are fully present and attentive.

- If you sense that you are missing important specific details in the communication, stop and tell the person the concepts and details that you did hear as a way to confirm that you are capturing the right meaning, especially if specific words seem to be important. This establishes a foundation for asking if there are additional specifics that are important for you to remember or give to others.

- Remember that words may be selected by the speaker for specific meaning, but in the context of his or her own motivational values. Ask yourself where the speaker is coming from (what motivates him/her) and how that could change the meaning. (See Chapter 19 for more on the tool of Using A Translator.)

* * * * *

The tool of Listening To Specific Word Choice can be uncomfortable for generalized listeners, but with practice, everyone can be better at capturing the details when it is important.

12. YOUR TONE OF VOICE TELLS ME SOMETHING DIFFERENT FROM YOUR WORDS
(*Tool #4 – Reading Meaning From Tone And Inflection*)

Words have definitions. The meaning is clear, at least to the speaker. But words alone cannot convey the full meaning of the sender. When we speak, we send both a verbal message and a companion non-verbal message. To be an effective receiver and fully understand a communication, we also need to understand the feeling or emotional content behind the words. Tone of voice and inflection convey additional meaning that puts the words into emotional context. Body language also sends an extraordinary amount of non-verbal information (as described in Chapter 13).

The words selected may have one meaning, say in an email. But words alone fall short of total communication. The same words in a phone or face-to-face conversation may mean exactly the opposite thing. Humor and sarcasm, especially sarcastic criticism, often depend on tone of voice and inflection.

Remember our definitions:

- Tone of voice – conveys the energy and mood behind the message (i.e., "Good morning" can be delivered with a tone that conveys real meaning – tired, bored, disinterested, happy, sad, excited, enthusiastic, sarcastic, angry, etc.).

- Inflection – places emphasis on specific words and indicates which words are most important in understanding the meaning (i.e., "*I* need you." vs. "I *need* you." vs. "I need *you*.")

Most of us are pretty good at picking up on the obvious – passion or enthusiasm, anger or loathing, sarcasm, and other extreme emotions. But many of us miss a lot of the deeper messages. Some of us do not look for deeper meaning in tone and inflection for many different reasons.

- Some people are oblivious or don't care enough to be bothered – "We've got a job to do, so let's get to it." Picking up on where someone is coming from gets in the way of the task.

- Other people, especially some people motivated by being self-contained, logical and right, believe that picking up the details of where someone is coming from can be a personal intrusion into the other person's life. It is rude or uncomfortable to be fully in tune with someone else's emotions.

Most of us are guilty of just being passive listeners in this area, thinking, "Listening is an activity." We pick up on the bigger or more extreme emotions, but miss the finer points.

It helps to remember that tone and inflection can be controlled, but generally reveal what the speaker is feeling or thinking. Most people reveal far more about what is behind the words than they imagine. We can improve our understanding tremendously if we can improve our ability to read the more subtle emotions reflected in tone of voice and inflection.

What's the point? If we are more effective listeners to tone and inflection, we will have a better idea of what we can expect from people, how motivated they are, how cooperative they are, how much they can be pushed, and so on. We will be more effective in knowing how to interact with people – whether we can jump to the task or whether we need to slow down and build them up before getting to the task.

Growing your skill in taking meaning from tone of voice and inflection requires paying closer attention to the speaker. We are more likely to miss the subtle changes in tone of voice and inflection if we are only a casual listener or multi-tasking. Your skill also improves if you use the Tool of Empathetic Listening (Chapters 15 and 16).

Now take a minute to think about how you use, or don't use the tool of reading tone and inflection. How can your listening improve if you make greater use of it? What are the personal benefits in your communication of being more aware of tone and inflection?

Here are a few tips from our training on being a more active listener for tone of voice and inflection. What else can you add that will help you personally?

- Remember that a better understanding of the emotional context of the words will help you understand what is being said and how to respond.

- Listen specifically for the level of energy in the words. It is a very effective way to listen *behind* the words.

- Pay attention to which words are emphasized in the communication.

- Combine what you hear in the tone and inflection with what people are doing as they speak or what their body language says. Look for support or contradiction. For example, low energy in the tone could be fatigue, but also could suggest mental or physical distraction as in the case of a person responding to you while he/she continues to read.

- Mentally relate the conversation to what you already know about the speaker as a person, and listen for tone and inflection that may relate to recent experiences or problems.

- If the tone or inflection does not seem to match the specific word choice or body language, ask yourself, "What are the dynamics here and how should I interact with this person?" Determine the best way to get to the root of what you heard in the non-verbal message.

- The tool of Being Fully Present (Chapter 8) will make you more aware of non-verbal communication and make it easier to pick up on the more subtle changes in tone of voice and inflection.

* * * * *

The tool of Reading Meaning From Tone And Inflection is easier to sharpen than many believe. Giving a person respect, applying the tools of Empathetic Listening, and Being Fully Present are foundations for building this skill.

13. BODY LANGUAGE?
THE ENGLISH LANGUAGE IS HARD ENOUGH
(*Tool #5 – Listening Without Words*)

Good listening goes beyond the words and the tone of voice or inflection. It includes all of the subtleties of reading body language.

Remember the definition of body language. Body language physically reveals what we are feeling or thinking. It is associated with the autonomic nervous system – we do it automatically, without thinking about it. It can be controlled (i.e., a poker face), but, generally, body language is an involuntary reflection of what we are thinking or feeling at the moment we are speaking. Think about what you do when you are on the phone. Your body is talking even when the person can't see you.

For many of us, most of our listening comes from the words and the tone of voice and inflection. We pick up additional meaning from the speaker's body language so that the body language flavors the meaning. It gives us a general approximation of the speaker's mindset, but the subtleties of body language are not part of the information in our listening. Body language has a secret message that many of us have not discovered yet or have not learned to utilize fully.

However, for some people, body language is more than important. It is an essential element of their listening. Some of these people get 50% or more of their listening information from the other person's body language. They could be described as watchers as much as listeners. The authors are on opposite ends of this spectrum. Laura seems to know what people are thinking just by reading body language even before listening to a few words. Olin depends primarily on words, tone of voice, and inflection. He has learned the value of reading body language and is learning, but will never totally master this innate gift. Several examples are in order.

- After a meeting of a board of directors, Laura was talking with the president about a potential problem – a point of resistance between the president and a board member. She said, "Did you see that body language? I think you have a problem." The president responded with a blank expression. "What body language?" Some people do not read or understand body language unless it is extreme.

- A typical conversation after we make a sales call or have a difficult client meeting generally goes something like this. Olin says, "I heard what they said, but what did they really say?" Laura will comment on where people were in agreement or disagreement, and how each person reacted to the meeting and where we may have a specific problem with each person. Reading body language brings great value to understanding any conversation or presentation.

- We were watching Colin Powell and the Prime Minister of Turkey on TV as they took questions from the press corps after a meeting prior to the Iraq war. Laura said, "They had a really difficult, strained meeting. Look at how tense they are. Look at how, even facing the press corps directly, they are facing slightly away from each other. Look at how they are subtly shouldering out of the conversation. Look at the tension between Powell's eyebrows, look at the stiffness of his eyebrows, and see that tension and fatigue in his eyes. Look at his tight upper lip. Do you see what he is doing with his fingers?" Olin looked at Powell's image and, not seeing many of the subtle movements, said, "I see a guy answering tough questions controlling his tone and inflection to be dispassionate." People who naturally read body language understand things that many of us miss. The words were putting a good face on an otherwise unsatisfactory meeting, but the body language told the real story. Future events bore out Laura's observations.

- We were presenting a proposal to two senior vice presidents to work with their board to help resolve deep-seated problems. One of the prospects asked how we would work with them and how we would know when a problem was developing. Laura said, "We have a lot of experience working with senior management teams. We'll just watch the interaction between you and head off the problem before it develops." He asked with a laugh, "How will you do that? Can you read our minds?" She answered, "I'll know by watching your body language as you work together." With disbelief, the prospect said, "OK. So tell me exactly what I am thinking right now!" She did, and he was astounded at the detail she gave on what he was feeling and thinking about the proposal, both positive and negative. His comment to Laura was a dismayed, "You get an A+." Pointing to the other vice president, he commanded, "Tell me what he's thinking!" At the end of the meeting, Laura noted with amusement that he turned his back to us and composed himself with a poker face before saying goodbye. Reading body language can be a true, innate gift that can scare people when fully revealed. The reaction in old Salem Massachusetts might have been to cry "Witch!" and grab some wood to start a fire around a stake.

People who naturally read body language at this level tend to be highly intuitive about people and are focused on relationships and helping or nurturing others. They take significant meaning from small movements in facial muscles and what appear to be small hand movements or posture changes. They tend to be highly sensitive to where people are coming from and pick up very quickly on the honesty, sincerity, and other feelings or motives behind the words. They often see the lie before it ever gets out of a speaker's mouth – they see it in the nonverbal communication.

How about some examples of meaning in body language?

- Putting your fingers around your mouth generally communicates that you are thinking about what is being said. One of our clients goes through an interesting change in body language as she listens and moves deeper and deeper into thought – hands around the chin, to fingers around the lips, to the index finger on the tip of her nose, to pushing her nose flat against her face. We know when we are connecting by where the fingers are. She was completely unaware that she did this and appreciated our making her aware of it.

- We were in a meeting with the CEO and several line managers. One difficult manager put her feet on an adjacent chair, turned her back to the CEO, and addressed both the group and the CEO. The body language was relaxed but clear – "Nobody in this room can touch me."

- A friend of ours was being confronted with a whole new way to think about an important part of his life. He sat sideways in the chair with his legs crossed away from the speaker, one shoulder turned into the group and speaker, and his face looking at the speaker. His body was faced out of the conversation with only one shoulder and his head engaged. His body language was shouting, "I'm here, but just barely. I'm highly skeptical. My head is listening, but I'm not sure I believe any of this stuff! And I'm ready for a very quick exit."

Now that you know what body language can be at close to a 100% level, you may want to reconsider how you rated your abilities in this area in the listening skills test on page 16.

Many of the people with the natural ability to read body language believe that everyone else has similar abilities, which can lead to real misunderstanding and conflict in communication. This explains the angry comment we sometimes hear, "If you don't know what the problem is, then you obviously don't care, and I won't tell you." These people are operating with the false premise that you have the ability to listen through body language. Because of this, they really do believe that you are insensitive and/or don't care.

In our training, we have found an unexpected contradiction. Many of the people with this gift of reading body language are better at reading what other people's bodies are saying than they are at thinking about the messages their own bodies are sending when they are talking or listening.

Sometimes there are real downsides to this natural gift of reading body language – it can interfere with the discussion and create a roadblock in the listening process. The listener with this ability may pick up on a problem that you are having in your life and be distracted from what you are saying. Another downside is that negative meaning can be taken where none is intended. The message received may be colored by the speaker's errant thoughts or attitude toward something else gong on in his/her life. This ability – reading body language – can make people more tentative or indirect in their interpersonal relationships. It may make it hard for them to delegate. For example, they can see what is really a minor momentary irritation, translate it into resistance, and withdraw the request. They are quick to perceive criticism where none was intended. They also tend to listen more for meaning and concept than specific word choice or details. They tend to be generalist listeners.

The purpose of this chapter is to help people who are not aware of the real power and true subtleties of body language to understand what they do not have and how easily people with this gift can read them. This book is not a book on body language, but we have included a few basics in the table on pages 62-64. Use these basics as a starting point, but always remember to look at the whole body in reading what is behind the words.

Those of us who do not have this natural ability probably never will be true masters of reading body language, but we can learn and be more effective. Here are a few tips that have worked. Add others that will help you.

- Find a good book on body language and study it. Learn what different body positions or motions mean.

- Think of body language as a foreign language. Learn the basic rules of meaning as if body motions or movements are foreign language words. Learn the definitions and rules of grammar (i.e., this body movement generally means …).

- Remember to put any one message in the context of the whole body. For example, a person sitting with his arms crossed may be resistive, but, if the rest of the body is relaxed, he/she could just be cold.

- Watch movies. Look at the character and ask yourself what the actor or actress is thinking or feeling. Then study changes in the position of the body, the facial muscle movements, the eyes and around the eyebrows, and the small hand motions. Try to relate the body language to the emotional message and how the emotional message conveys meaning through the body language. Acting is the art of body language. Apply two caveats to this tip. First, much of the body language is overdone to ensure that the whole audience gets it. Second, this suggestion applies to the best of Hollywood. Some actors or actresses never really get into their character emotionally and have little to teach you about body language.

- Try watching your own body language as you talk. Tie changes in what you are thinking to changes in your position, arm or hand movements, and so on.

- Find someone who naturally reads body language and ask him or her to be your personal tutor. Ask them to explain, in detail, what they are taking from a conversation and the specific body language that gives them this message. This probably is the best approach because only someone with the innate ability can teach the subtleties. How do you find that person? Use the *Sources of Information in Listening* test on page 13 to help identify the right person. Remember that many people who read body language naturally will have to stop to think about how they really do listen and what they get from body language. They typically assume the rest of the world reads body language the way they do.

* * * * *

The tool of Listening Without Words, or reading body language, is either an innate gift or a learned skill for you. It is a powerful tool that will give you tremendous insight into where people are coming from when they are talking and how you are being received when you are talking. It will give you information and sensitivities to make your interaction with people more effective. Of the authors, Laura wonders how people can survive without it, and Olin has discovered both how hard it is to learn at the more subtle levels and how valuable it is to catching the communication pass. Both of the authors recommend that you invest in growing this skill.

Reading body language is an exercise in subtleties. No single body position or movement alone tells the full story. A single body motion needs to be read in the context of the rest of the body as well as the words, tone, and inflection. The following are a few basics to get you started. Be careful not to apply body language guidelines as absolutes. Put everything in context and remember that some people have movements that are unique to them and their emotions.

Eyes – First, watch the eyes:

- The eyes are the window to the soul.
- Is the person making direct eye contact with you during the conversation? If not, they probably are hiding something – anger, disrespect, dishonesty, boredom, shyness, uncertainty, physical attraction, etc.
- Is there eye contact when the other person is speaking? If no, *always* ask yourself what he/she is hiding.
- What emotion is showing in the eyes – sincerity, joy, fear, uncertainty, calculation, surprise, anger, etc.?
- Are the eyes open or narrowed? Narrowed eyes suggest anger or deviousness.
- Did the eyes open wide? Wide open eyes may indicate surprise or astonishment.
- If the eyes are cold, you may have an enemy.

Face – Second, watch the face:

- Is the face relaxed or tense?
- Especially look for tension or emotion around the eyes, eyebrows, forehead, and mouth. When a person is upset, the face tends to freeze or tense.
- Is he/she facing you squarely? If no, ask yourself how fully present they are.

Head – The head often shows mental engagement:

- What is the position and angle of the head? Forward says thoughtful, back says disengaged, to the side suggests engaged but not convinced.
- The angle of the head may indicate differing degrees of thoughtfulness.
- Forehead leading suggests deep concentration.
- If the chin is leading, you are facing resistance.

Hands – Hands add to the message

- Relaxed hands indicate that everything is OK.
- Are the fingers moving? Fingers tend to start moving when people are thinking, impatient, or nervous.
- How much tension is in the hands? The more tension or clenching, the greater the resistance. Fully clenched hands say significant anger and conflict.
- Are fingers near the mouth? This indicates that the person is thinking.
- A finger on the lips suggests formulation of a question, especially pursed lips.
- Is a hand near the forehead masking the eyes? This may indicate being overwhelmed or in need of pause to catch up, especially if taking notes. Things are proceeding too fast to process.
- Is a hand supporting the weight of the head? This suggests fatigue, boredom, or a fried brain.

Arms – Are the arms crossed?

- Are the arms crossed over the chest? This generally indicates resistance or defiance. However, if the rest of the body language is relaxed, the person may be cold or physically uncomfortable.
- Big men in small chairs frequently cross their arms over their chest as they try to adjust their bodies to the chair. Crossed arms could mean that you should invest in more comfortable chairs.
- Check the overall body language for context.

Overall body language – This defines the context for specific body parts:

- How relaxed and open is the overall body? The more open, the more receptive.
- How much energy is the body showing?
- Is the other person's body facing you squarely or turned to side? A squarely positioned body indicates openness or directness and full engagement.
- Has the person put a shoulder between the two of you? That person is distancing himself/herself from you. It shows resistance or skepticism.
- Crossing of a leg toward you enters the person into the conversation. The leg crossed away takes him/her out of the conversation. When watching crossed legs, remember that crossed legs get tired after a while and will be moved. The initial crossing is the most telling.
- Is the body sitting forward or back in relation to the chair? Forward shows interest. Back shows desire for control, lack of interest, resignation, disengagement, or simply fatigue.
- When a person is standing, is the body relaxed or tensed? A fully engaged open person will meet you directly with relaxed body language. In direct confrontation the body tends to be squared and weight balanced, but with a tension present in the body language. If the body is not faced into the conversation, then resistance, disagreement, impatience, or boredom may be present. Bottom line – the person is not fully invested in the conversation.

14. I THINK THIS IS WHAT YOU MEANT
(*Tool #6 – Confirmation*)

How often do we find that we truly do not understand what the other person means, especially when talking about complex ideas, difficult concepts, or emotional situations? We hesitate to interrupt, confess incomplete understanding (or bewilderment), and ask what they really meant. Who wants to look like an idiot? So we take the road of assuming instead of confirming, and sometimes pay the consequences.

We are pretty good listeners, but sometimes the communication process breaks down. Why does this happen? What's the problem? How can we ensure complete communication *as a listener* and not come off looking like a complete idiot?

Several factors may be at work, either independently or together. We each have our own set of things that get in the way of fully understanding. Here are a few examples.

- We are being forced to deal with too much of something – too much data, too much emotional content or feelings, too much change, too much flexibility. We all have a "too much" category that bogs us down as listeners.

- The other person is having trouble communicating – poorly worded or awkwardly stated ideas, or there is uncertainty in the delivery.

- We may be filtering out some information that we naturally consider to be less important based on what motivates us (as described in Chapter 5).

- The same words mean different things to different people. Sometimes the meanings are remarkably different. We think we are communicating, but somehow we have missed. (See Chapter 6 for a more complete explanation.)

- We may have disengaged mentally to think about our response or what to do with part of the information transmitted (as described in Chapter 10).

- Our mind works faster than people can communicate, and it is easy to wander off mentally. Something triggers an errant thought. We suddenly find ourselves somewhere out in left field or maybe even on another planet. We desperately need a polite way back into the conversation.

Whatever the reason, ensuring our complete understanding is important. How do we do this? The answer is simple. *Restate your understanding in words that mean something to you.* This approach uses the tool of Confirmation. It is a tactful way to ensure that we have the information or understanding that we need.

The tool of Confirmation is no more than asking yourself if you truly understand, at a detailed level, everything that you need to know. If the answer is no, restate what you think the speaker meant. Examples:

- "Let me summarize what you have said."

- "This is really interesting (or revealing, or helpful, or whatever). What you are saying is …."

- "I see what you mean. You are saying …"

- "OK. I see what I (or we) need to be doing. It is …"

This tool provides added value to the conversation in several ways:

- It reinforces our involvement in the conversation, shows respect for the speaker's ideas, and helps us be fully present.

- It confirms meaning. If the speaker had something else in mind, the conversation can take a side step to ensure more complete communication.

- It gives you the opportunity to expand or build on the idea or to work suggested remedies or actions into the conversation. We can confirm understanding and build at the same time.

- It is an effective way to come along side someone conversationally to show that you agree with part of what was said and then move the person in a slightly different direction.

- It is a polite way to reenter the conversation if we have drifted away and, at the same time, it shows that we have been engaged up to that point.

- The key to success with this listening tool is to use it tactfully. If the request for confirmation is too direct, it can put people on the defensive.

People who are motivated by helping and nurturing others sometimes are uncomfortable in using this tool for several reasons. First, they may feel foolish because they have not understood the message on the first try. Second, people with these motivational values sometimes work hard to avoid conflict and loss of harmony. They may avoid confirmation when they have just gotten through a sticky wicket because they might discover that the wicket is still sticky – that they really haven't resolved things and some point of disagreement or conflict still remains. Or, based on the subtleties of non-verbal communication, they may conclude that they do not have complete agreement and not use the tool of confirmation in order to avoid conflict. Unfortunately, this choice leaves issues unresolved and rarely achieves anything except a false appearance of harmony. Third, asking directly for confirmation may appear to them to be somewhat rude and pushy.

What is the point? If you use this tool correctly, you will not have false starts or unnecessary conflict because of your incomplete understanding. Here are a few suggestions we have picked up to help you feel more comfortable or confident in using the tool of Confirmation. Add to them or modify them to fit who you are.

- Remember that this is a personal mindset issue. The speaker usually *wants* you to understand. The person sending the message generally is willing to take a side step in the conversation to ensure that you understand. Therefore, the real issue may be how comfortable you are in using the tool of Confirmation.

- During the conversation, ask yourself what are the consequences of a misunderstanding or incomplete understanding. Use the tool of Confirmation as needed. This downside appraisal can give you greater courage to use it.

- Remember that most people underutilize this tool. You can use it more liberally than you think, but be tactful rather than blunt when using it.

- If you think you are overusing this tool and may be starting to look like an idiot in the speaker's eyes, consider modifying how you use it. Combine confirming and expanding or building on the idea or solutions by adding your thoughts. For example: "This is a really tough problem. The things we need to address are … and here are some alternative approaches." The "alternative approaches" are your add to what you heard.

- Watch out for people who withdraw from the conversation in disgust because you didn't get it the first time. They may simply agree that you heard correctly even if you really did not understand. Use tone, inflection, and body language to determine if you are getting a true "yes" and hold your ground until you have complete understanding.

- Evaluate the situation. Some circumstances complicate the use of this tool – where there are time issues (the boss or family member is headed out the door and already is late); where the speaker has been difficult, strong-willed, or belligerent in the conversation; or in other "non-normal" situations. Apply your best judgment and emotional intelligence. Tailor the timing or use of this tool accordingly. But also recognize that sometimes you have to fight for understanding and demand time because the consequences of not understanding have significant negative consequences.

- Remember the importance of tact. Being tactful shows respect. If you are too blunt in your verbal *and* non-verbal message, it may come across as criticism ("What a stupid idea!"), especially if the other person is struggling with communicating the message.

- Consider ending conversations or meetings with this tool. It will help get you into the practice of using it more effectively during a conversation.

- Never assume. Always confirm.

*   *   *   *   *

The tool of Confirmation is a powerful tool to enhance meaning and is easy to use. Using this tool is more a function of your comfort and making it a personal listening habit than anything else.

15. PUT YOURSELF IN THE OTHER PERSON'S SHOES
(Tool #7 – Empathetic Listening – Part 1)

What is the personal context? What is the other person really thinking or feeling? What has he or she gone through or experienced? These things are real and put the other person's words in a true personal context.

While some of us react by saying, "So what's the big deal? I just need to know what they said. I don't have time for a lot of emotional fluffy stuff." Others respond, "How can you ignore these things? They're more important than the words. *They may be more important than life itself.*"

All of these things, and more, are part of the conversation. They underlie the words and provide meaning to what the speaker is saying. They are there for us as listeners if we use the tool of Empathetic Listening.

Empathetic listening is a state of mind. It is putting yourself in the other person's shoes and understanding the world as he or she may see it. Empathetic listening goes beyond the words and specific word choice. Here is where non-verbal communication – tone of voice, inflection, and body language – comes into play and provides important additional meaning. But empathetic listening goes beyond receiving the verbal and non-verbal communication. It combines and integrates verbal and non-verbal communication with the personal knowledge we have about people. It puts the message into the speaker's personal context.

As listeners, we need to think about *who* the speaker is and *where* he or she is coming from. This mindset is at the heart of using the tool of Empathetic Listening. Examples of things you should be considering include:

- What is the reason behind the conversation? Is the intent honest and sincere or are there other motives?

- What motivates or builds the self-worth of this person? Are they motivated by getting into action, by helping others, by being logical and right, or by being included in the group and building consensus?

- What is the speaker's personal situation at home and work, regardless of whether it relates to the specific topic being discussed?

- What has this person experienced recently? Is the person going through (or recently gone through) a personal crisis? Is the speaker demotivated or burned out at home or at work? Was there a recent job or personal success (promotion, raise, new assignment, engagement or marriage, new house, etc.) or failure (termination, lost sale, difficulty with boss, financial problems, someone took credit for his/her work, etc.)?

- What is the intelligence level (IQ and emotional intelligence)? What is the level of education, training, or relevant life experience?

Listening empathetically has special value. It helps us to know *how* to listen better to the speaker. Empathetic listening helps us listen for meaning that we otherwise might not hear. It adds special and unique meaning to the communication received. We are listening not only for information, but also for how people have been or will be affected. We are in a better position to draw them out for more complete communication. It also helps us respond in a more positive and productive way – words, tone, inflection, and body language. For example, a speaker's transmission alone might normally warrant a "that's nice" type answer. The same communication using the tool of Empathetic Listening could warrant an entirely different response.

Most of us look at life primarily from our own point of view. If we do this, it tends to limit our perspectives. Therefore, the power of empathetic listening brings two benefits. First, it is an important part of understanding the other person. It also gives us a more personal lasting benefit. It broadens our life view and enlarges our life experiences. We see life from a different perspective, which enriches our own life and stimulates different ways of thinking.

Now take a minute. Put the power of empathetic listening in your own personal context. Think about who you are and the personal circumstances that underlie your communication. How do you feel when someone ignores what you think is important or where you are coming from? How do you feel when people appear to be insensitive to some change in your life circumstances? For some of us, the answer might be, "Hey! No big deal. Let's get on with what we're doing. We can't take time for a bunch of emotional hand holding right now." Others are thinking, "It's none of your business" or "What an invasion of privacy." Now think about how you would feel if another person made a point of understanding these things about us and then treated us accordingly, even if your first inclination was "No big deal" or "None of your business." Even the "Hey – no big deal" or "None of your business" types respond in a more positive way to someone who is an empathetic listener and invests the effort to know what is important in their lives.

Empathetic listening is not just being sensitive to personal issues and situations. It also includes being sensitive to other people's motivational values – what motivates them and enhances their sense of self-worth. If you know what is important to someone in terms of motivational values (getting into action, helping others, being self-reliant and "right", being part of the group, etc.), then you may listen for different things or be more sensitive to nuances and subtleties in certain areas. This is empathetic listening carried to a high level.

Where are you strong or weak at putting yourself in the other person's shoes? What does that mean for you in improving as an empathetic listener? Here are a few suggestions for making better use of the tool of Empathetic Listening. Think about how to apply this tool more effectively from your own perspective and create additional tips for yourself.

- Remember that empathetic listening is all about your personal mindset as a listener. It is a decision only you can make to be more intelligent as a listener.

- Consider what motivates you and how your own motivational values may get in the way of being a better empathetic listener.

- Try to recognize and remember what appears to motivate people when you are talking with them. Adjust your listening as appropriate – to the importance of being in action, being helpful, being right, and building consensus.

- Use your imagination to imagine how you might feel if you had experienced the same positive or negative situation, but always remember that everyone has his/her own perceptual filters and motivational values, and that each of us reacts in different ways.

- Remember that there are different levels of directness in natural communication styles. Some people are direct, almost to the point of being perceived as rude. Others are so indirect that the answer of "yes" to a question might actually be said as "that might be nice." This is part of empathetic listening.

- Remember that a person's life situation and emotional condition have a real impact on what they may mean or intend as well as what contributes to personal demotivation and burnout.

- Remember how good it feels to have someone truly understand where you are coming from and consider your personal situation or condition in conversations *where it is appropriate*.

- Empathetic listening shows respect for the other person – that we are trying to be considerate of all of the things that are influencing a person's communication.

- Recognize that the failure to use this tool can result in demotivation, stress, conflict, and other negative outcomes. What we hear and how we respond verbally and non-verbally have a positive or negative emotional and motivational impact on the speaker.

*   *   *   *   *

The tool of Empathetic Listening adds tremendously to your understanding and can help create a sense of personal bond or loyalty if you want one. This tool is difficult for many to master and use consistently. It is easier to master if you already are intuitive about people. For the rest of us, it requires getting over the sense that we are invading someone's personal emotional space or it requires making empathetic listening part of the task.

16. LISTEN WITH AN EAR FOR CULTURAL, REGIONAL, AND GENDER DIFFERENCES
(Tool #7 - Empathetic Listening – Part 2)

We are all different, and we hear it expressed in so many different ways. Some are stereotypes, but others are very real.

> "I'm from a small town in the Mid-west.
> Those New Yorkers just drive me up the wall."
>
> "Hey! I'm Italian (or choose your own culture)
> and grew up in an Italian neighborhood. What can I say?!"
>
> "Men are from Mars. Women are from Venus."
>
> "Direct eye contact is considered rude or confrontational in our culture."

We are all individuals and different in what motivates us and enhances our self-esteem (as described in previous chapters). But we also bring differences and sensitivities to the communication process because of our genders and regional or cultural backgrounds.

As listeners, we need to be sensitive to these differences. These differences underlie our communications. They can influence the meaning of our communications at all levels – words, tone, inflection, and body language. These differences apply both to sending and receiving. They affect what we say and how we say it. They also affect the filter we wear when listening.

Good listeners extend the tool of Empathetic Listening to gender and regional or cultural differences. Good listeners also recognize the fundamental problems of communicating across language barriers, where one person may be using English as a second language, or where you are using a second language.

Where do you have specific issues? What additional things can you do to deal with these problems?

Here are a few tips for improving in this area and extending the tool of Empathetic Listening.

- Remember that listening with an ear for gender and regional or cultural differences is a mindset. It is a decision to take yourself and what you are hearing out of your personal context and put it into a different context.

- Think of the other person as different, and put a priority on honoring the differences. Good communication comes from celebrating differences rather than ignoring them or being in conflict over them. This is another way of respecting the person as a human being, but with a greater degree of sophistication.

- Recognize that there are significant differences between the Americanized version of a culture (Italian-American, Japanese-American, etc.) and what you will encounter in another country. If you are dealing internationally, find information about the specific cultural differences and educate yourself. Americans tend to be known around the world as culturally self-centered (another stereotype?). To be successful, it is important to make a sincere attempt to understand the differences.

- Consider reading a book on relationships between men and women, but remember that generalizations are always wrong. Men are not always from Mars and women are not always from Venus. Our culture may establish perceptual stereotypes, but what motivates people and builds their self worth (being in action, nurturing or helping, being logical and right, and being part of the group and building consensus) is not determined by gender.

- Keep things in balance. Being sensitive to these issues doesn't mean losing your sense of self. The objective is not to become a member of the other culture. It is more a matter of recognizing the differences as you listen as a matter of respect.

*   *   *   *   *

Extending the tool of Empathetic Listening across gender as well as regional and cultural boundaries requires more of an effort to get out of ourselves, but adds real meaning and additional insight into the other person's communication to us and broadens our own perceptions and ways of thinking.

17. EYE CONTACT WHEN *YOU* ARE TALKING MAKES *YOU* A BETTER LISTENER
(*Tool #8 – Eye Contact When Talking*)

Listening is more than hearing and understanding the speaker's words. We need to understand *where* they are coming from and *how* they are relating in the two-way communication process.

How are they reacting to what you said? Remember, communication is a dynamic process. We react to their words, and they react to our words. Did they understand what we said? Were they confused? Were they disinterested or bored? What the other person is feeling or thinking about our words is important to really understand the meaning of their response.

An important part of *our* listening is watching their reaction to our ideas and messages. This means that eye contact is important when sending as well as receiving.

Most of us are pretty good at eye contact when the other person is talking. Many of us need to work on eye contact when we are talking. We often catch ourselves looking off in another direction or avoiding direct eye contact when we are speaking. Ask yourself these simple questions. The answer to these questions makes keeping some kind of eye contact important to us personally.

- How can I possibly understand what they are thinking and their mindset when they respond to me if I'm not watching their faces when I speak?

- What reaction did I miss while my eyes were off somewhere else?

- What unintended message am I sending to them with my poor eye contact when speaking? Remember, your poor eye contact is a non-verbal suggestion that you have something to hide.

Many people feel uncomfortable making direct eye contact throughout a conversation. A few of the reasons for poor eye contact when we are talking include:

- Direct eye contact can be distracting to you as a speaker, especially if you are highly intuitive and receive so many non-verbal messages from the other person.

- Some of us avoid eye contact because we do not want to appear too confrontational or domineering when talking.

- Constant direct eye contact can be very uncomfortable because the eyes are the window to the heart and soul, and we don't want to reveal too much of ourselves except to special relationships.

- Our own uncertainty may cause us to look off in another direction while we are thinking – kind of an eye contact hesitation.

- Our intentions are not pure or our communication is not honest, and we are hiding our intentions or dishonesty.

- We are embarrassed, shy, or introverted.

- We don't want to see a negative reaction that we may have to deal with.

Think about your eye contact practices when talking. Characterize the situations where you can maintain eye contact when talking and where you are less successful. Add your own personal reasons to this list.

The real issue for us is how to read the other person's *face* while we are talking and still be comfortable in the conversation. Here are a few suggestions for improving your eye contact when talking. Add others that apply to you and will help you in this area based on situations that give you difficulty.

- Remember, their reaction to your words will color your understanding as you listen. You are *watching* to listen for problems in the speaker's response – are there points of resistance or confusion, where do you need to elaborate, etc.?

- Keep in mind that you are sending an unintentional message with poor eye contact when you are speaking. The primary message is lack of respect, but remember that poor eye contact often suggests that you are trying to hide something – your honesty, your sincerity or true intent, your anger or disdain, your disgust, your uncertainty, your self-confidence, etc.

- Watch their faces without direct eye-to-eye contact. Remember that the objective is to watch the body language in their faces not to read their heart and soul with a piercing stare. This approach is effective, especially if you receive too many distracting non-verbal messages by maintaining eye contact.

- Practice watching your listener's facial reactions, but without direct eye contact. Focus near the eye – nose, chin, or forehead. Hold the direct eye contact for when you want to stress a specific point.

- Remember that face contact sends the message that you are part of the conversation. So at the very least, give face contact instead of looking away.

- As a test for how well you are doing, especially with people that you are meeting for the first time, make sure you know the color of the other person's eyes.

*   *   *   *   *

The tool of Eye Contact When Talking can be quite difficult to master and use consistently. In part, it is a matter of self-confidence. It also is understanding what the other person's body is saying. Once mastered, you probably will find that you have more control over the conversation for two reasons. First, you will be getting information that is lost now even if you have only limited skill in reading body language. Secondly, you will appear more confident and commanding – eye contact in delivery always carries with it the aura of confidence in what you are saying.

18. LISTEN WITH YOUR BODY
(*Tool #9 – Using Your Body To Be A Better Listener*)

Imagine yourself making a presentation or talking with several people. One person is leaning forward, fingers around her mouth. Another is leaning back, arms crossed. A third person is listening, but doodling on a pad of paper. How are you doing? Who is listening and catching your communication pass? Who might be reacting negatively? Who is taking it in, thinking about it, and understanding what you are saying?

Now think about your own body language *when you listen*. Your body is talking too. What do people typically see? Are people likely to say that you *look* like you are fully present and taking it in, or that you are disinterested or somewhere else?

Remember that body language follows our mind. It unconsciously communicates what we are thinking and feeling. If we don't look like we are listening, we probably are not, or at least we are not listening completely. Your body language is communicating to the speaker how effectively you are listening as well as how you may be interpreting or reacting to the speaker's message. Your body language also is communicating how much or little you respect the other person.

We can make a conscious decision to pay closer attention and become more engaged in the conversation. Our body language immediately reflects the change in our listening behavior. Alternatively, we can find ourselves drifting out of a conversation and proactively decide to rearrange our body into a more positive listening position – head forward, body forward, fingers around the mouth, no body parts between us and the speaker, face square to the speaker, etc. Sometimes our hands are twiddling with clothing and the only way to stop is to put our hands together. The very process of changing our listening position can have a positive impact on our mental commitment to listening more closely. And our listening improves.

Positive *listening* body language not only facilitates our listening, but also contributes to a more positive personal interaction. Good listening posture tells the speaker that you are "getting it" and that he/she can move on with confidence. The speaker will feel less compelled to repeat what was said or go into more detail or give more examples to ensure that the message is received and understood. What is the benefit to us? Shorter conversations, time saved, more motivated employees and team members, and better relationships with friends and family members.

Here are a few tips to making more effective use of your own body language as a listening tool. What can you add that will help you?

- Think of this tool as a matter of mind over body.

- Arrange yourself into a listening position at the beginning of any conversation. Avoid a slouching and laid back posture.

- Watch your body language as you listen. Ask yourself why your body language has changed. It may help you deal more effectively with the incoming information or ask questions to clarify. Have you crossed your arms across your chest or closed your fists? You may be resisting the information or starting into stress or conflict. Have you slouched back in your chair? You may be losing interest. Certainly your body is talking, and you are communicating a change in your listening behavior.

- When you catch yourself not understanding completely, picking up only part of the information, or drifting out of a conversation, say to yourself, "I will give the speaker my full undivided attention!" and, surprisingly your body language will change. Or if you are having trouble really being interested, make a physical change to a more attentive listening posture. It should improve your listening effectiveness.

- Think about your listening body language in the context of respecting the other person. The speaker is deserving of your respect as a human being if for no other reason. Arranging and controlling your body language as a listener is one form of respect. It is part of being fully present while listening.

*   *   *   *   *

The tool of Listening With Your Body requires being aware of your own body language more than anything else. It pays big dividends in how effective we are in capturing more information and contributing to our being fully present.

19. YOU DIDN'T REALLY MEAN WHAT I HEARD YOU SAY
(*Tool #10 – Using A Translator To Take The Sting Out Of Words*)

Sometimes we find ourselves reacting negatively to a person's word choice and dropping or lunging into stress or conflict, but then discover that there was no real issue once we get to the bottom of it. It was a simple, but sometimes painful, miscommunication. This kind of conflict is unwarranted because we agree on the objective. The conflict comes from poor communication – receiving a poorly thrown communication pass and reacting in a negative way. These misunderstandings can create problems, waste time, and consume emotional energy. Some sources estimate that as much as 80% of the conflict in our lives is unwarranted conflict.

The problem generally boils down to a few simple issues that were discussed in earlier chapters.

- We are motivated by different things – getting into action, helping others, being logical and right, or being included in the group and getting consensus.

- The same words mean different things to different people, and the differences often relate to differences in motivational values. These differences in meaning are significant.

- We understand that we are different, but we forget these differences in communicating.

- We listen through our own motivational values and filters, as though everyone is speaking the same language.

Misunderstandings from these fundamental issues come in a variety of sizes and shapes, and these misunderstandings depend very much on the motivational values of the people in the conversation. The solution is to take a breath and turn on your translator to take the sting out of the words. Two examples should make the point.

Someone who is motivated by getting into immediate action and task completion says to an analytical person, who is motivated by having lots of data, being logical, and being right, "I don't care what, this task has to be finished by next Friday!" What message did the analytical person probably hear? "Quality, logic, and good analysis don't matter. Take shortcuts and get the job done even if it's wrong!" This message attacks the analytical person's sense of self-worth at the core and could plunge him or her into conflict. Now let's use the translator. The analytical person takes a breath and says to himself or herself, "He didn't really mean what I heard him say. He's one of those 'let's get into action types'. What is he really saying? He wants the job done by Friday, but he expects me to take care of the details and get it done right." Now the conversation can take a more positive direction and not start with conflict. The two people can discuss what needs to be done in a more rational way.

A nurturing person who is motivated by helping others and maintaining a harmonious conflict-free environment says to someone motivated by getting into action, "We can't just charge ahead without thinking about people's reaction and considering how Sally and Fred feel about this." The charge-ahead person immediately sees a barrier to getting into action and probably hears something like, "We have to consider *everyone's* feelings and spend all sorts of *wasted time* patting people on the hands. This is going to take forever. We'll *never* get this thing going." Conflict can be immediate and detrimental. Now let's turn on the translator. Action Jackson takes a breath and says to herself, "He didn't really mean what I heard. He's one of those 'nurturing types' and has good intuition about people. What he is really saying is that there will be problems implementing this change, and it could actually slow down the process unless we get the people on board." Now the conversation can turn to the people problems and how to deal with them while still staying on schedule.

We could cite many more examples. Instead, think up a few examples on your own. Consider how people with different motivational values might express themselves and apply word meaning and listening filters. What should the listener be thinking when the translator is turned on? Refer to Chapter 5 – We Don't Hear What We Filter Out – for a reminder on how people with different motivational values listen.

There are other reasons to use the translator beyond differences in motivational values. Sometimes people are just awkward or clumsy in throwing the communication pass. Not all of us express ourselves in the most effective or positive ways. Sometimes we are insensitive to a person's personal situation, and they react negatively. Try to be forgiving as a listener and step beyond the words. Remember the Golden Rule – Do to others, as we would like others to do to us when we are awkward or unintentionally insensitive – be understanding.

Use the tool of the Translator in putting the verbal message into context beyond differences in motivational values. Use non-verbal communication to try to understand the speaker's intention. Did they intend to be confrontational or rude, or was it just awkward or unintentional.

The tool of using a translator is very effective. It helps us to (1) better understand what people are really saying and (2) take the sting out of words. People with different motivational values really do speak different languages, even though we all use the English language.

Here are a few suggestions for being more effective using your translator.

- Remember that different people have different meanings for the same word.

- Remember that people perceive the world differently and are motivated by different things. These perceptions and values are not right or wrong. They are just different.

- Don't be frustrated by the differences. Each set of motivational values brings its own unique strengths and weakness.   Recognize the differences and the value each brings, and celebrate the differences. Use the differences to strengthen your team or family and improve the outcome.

- Remember that most people are better listeners if they are not in conflict. It usually is more productive to control your reaction and stay out of conflict.

- When you hear something that creates challenge, anger, or demotivation, don't react immediately. First, stop to take a breath and then consider that the motivational values of the speaker may be different. Turn on your translator. Then ask questions or turn the conversation to confirm the intended meaning.

- Remember the importance of respect. We are all different. Each person is deserving of respect as a human being even if he/she is different from us.

*   *   *   *   *

The tool of Using A Translator requires effort to understand other people and what motivates them and then apply high levels of emotional intelligence. It also requires some empathetic listening (where are people coming from). This may be one of the more difficult tools to use consistently, but the rewards are great – better understanding and less stress and conflict in your life.

20. A FIVE-STEP PLAN TO IMPROVE YOUR LISTENING SKILLS
(*The 11ᵗʰ tool – Testing And Focusing Your Improvement Efforts*)

You now understand the verbal and non-verbal components of listening and your preferred sources of information when listening. You understand the kinds of filters people put on their listening and how that can be tied to what motivates each individual. You have measured your listening skills and know how close you are to being a 100% listener – you have some metrics. You also have 10 powerful listening tools and some 70 tips on how to use these tools to improve your listening skills.

Mastering these 10 tools will empower you to become a 100% listener. As a recap, the 10 listening tools are:

The 10 Listening Tools

1. Being fully present
2. Controlled verbal and mental response
3. Listening specifically to word choice
4. Reading meaning from tone and inflection
5. Listening without words – reading body language
6. Confirmation
7. Empathetic listening
8. Eye contact when talking
9. Using your body to be a better listener
10. Using a translator to take the sting out of words

You have new knowledge! What are you going to do with it? Confucius said that "The essence of knowledge is, having it, using it."

It's easy to say, "I am going to improve my listening." The question is, how can you be systematic and hold yourself accountable? We have a five-step plan for you as well as a few suggestions on how to be more effective in holding yourself accountable.

1. Retake the *Are You A 100% Listener* test now that you understand more of the implications and ramifications of the 10 listening questions. Use pages 96 and 97.

2. Revisit the list of personal benefits on page 10 to reconfirm the "it needs to matter to me personally" issue.

3. Make a list of all of the things that you can do to improve in each of the areas of listening. Use the grid on pages 94 and 95 as a worksheet.

4. Choose the listening skill that you rated lowest, or a low rated skill that is very important to you. Make a specific plan to improve in that area over the next 30 days. Your list of improvement actions from step three is your guide to what you should be doing.

5. Retake the listening skills test at the end of 30 days. How did you do? Move on to the next lowest or next most important listening skill for you and repeat step four. Continue on for six months. Use the form on pages 98 and 99 to keep your scores and measure your progress each month.

If you follow this simple five-step process, the results will surprise and delight you. We use the same process in our training.

You will be more effective in growing your listening skills if you can find a way to hold yourself accountable for your growth as a listener. This is a matter of emotional intelligence, and we have a few suggestions to help you.

- Write down your specific commitment for the month on a file card or sticky note page. Leave the note strategically placed so that you will see it several times a day. It will be a regular reminder to focus on your objective.

- Keep a journal. You may find it helpful to document your objective and then take two or three minutes to jot down how you did each day and what you can do tomorrow to be more effective in meeting your growth objective. Being aware that you will make an entry in the journal at the end of each day will help you hold yourself accountable throughout the day.

- Ask another person to hold you accountable. Meet or talk for a few minutes once a week to discuss how you are doing and how you could do better. If the other person also is working on his/her listening skills, you can hold each other accountable.

In holding ourselves accountable, we create deadlines for growth and are less likely either to put off specific efforts to improve or to be content with the general knowledge of better listening skills and forget about the effort to really grow. The process of retaking the listening skills test every month will help you hold yourself accountable at the same time you are measuring your progress. It reinforces your commitment to grow – success breeds success.

So what? You invest the time and learn how to use the 10 listening tools. What are the personal benefits in using these tools? You will find that you:

- Understand more;

- Save time;

- Have shorter, more effective conversations;

- Resolve conflict faster and more effectively;

- Avoid conflict from misunderstanding what people are saying;

- Find that people think you are smarter and more sincere;

- Have richer personal and professional relationships;

- Gain opportunities for greater personal and professional growth and advancement.

Do we ever get there – to be a 100% listener? We teach listening skills and practice what we preach. We have found that, no matter how good you are, there always is room for improvement. The more we work on our listening skills, the more we learn about the subtleties of being a truly effective listener. We continue to grow and learn and take our listening to even greater levels.

We wish you the greatest success on the road to becoming a 100% listener. You no longer need to be part of a nation of incomplete listeners.

WORKSHEETS

ACTIONS TO IMPROVE MY LISTENING SKILLS

For each of the key listening skills, write specific actions that you can take to improve. Especially consider those areas (according to your *Are You A 100% Listener?* test) where you scored lower.

KEY LISTENING AREAS	WHAT I WILL DO TO IMPROVE
Being fully present and communicating your interest in listening	
Waiting to start talking	
Listening to understand fully vs. shutting down to plan your response	
Listening for specific word choices vs. general meaning	
Tone of voice / inflection	
Reading body language	
Paraphrasing to confirm understanding	

Putting yourself in other person's shoes (empathetic listening)	
Listening for cultural, regional, gender differences	
Eye contact when talking	
Using your body to be a better listener	
Using your translator	

MEASURING YOUR IMPROVEMENT AS A LISTENER OVER TIME
Are You A 100% Listener?

Please rate yourself on a scale of 1 to 10 (10 = highest) in the following areas every 30 days and record the results on pages 98 and 99.

	QUESTIONS	In Comfort Zone	In Stress Zone
1	How much do you pay attention to specific word choices and nuances when you are listening (vs. just listening for general meaning)?		
2	How much do you pay attention to the other person's tone of voice or inflection when listening?		
3	How often do you wait for the other person to finish talking completely before you start talking? At the highest level (10), there actually might be a slight pause in the conversation before you start to talk.		
4	How well do you maintain eye or face contact (the ability to watch the other person's facial reaction) when you are talking?		
5	How well do you understand *and* read body language?		

6	How much do you listen to understand fully what the other person is saying (vs. listening only partially and thinking of what you will say or how you will respond when the other person stops talking)?		
7	How often do you paraphrase what the other person says or ask a question to ensure your understanding before continuing the conversation, particularly for more difficult ideas or when someone is upset or angry?		
8	How often do you put yourself in other people's shoes, listening empathetically to understand how they feel or where they are coming from (i.e., emotionally, logically, or experientially)?		
9	How much do you listen for different meanings or messages based on cultural, regional, or gender differences?		
10	How well do you communicate your interest in listening (i.e., your body language or verbal acknowledgment of what the other person is saying)?		
	TOTAL	%	%

How did you rate yourself?

90 to 100% – Either outstanding or who are you kidding?;
80 to 90% – Very good listener; **70 to 80%** – Good listener;
60 to 70% – Average listener; **50 to 60%** – Fair listener, need work;
40 to 50% – Poor listener, really need work;
Less than 40% – What did they say?

MEASURING YOUR IMPROVEMENT AS A LISTENER OVER TIME

Record the scores from the *Are You A 100% Listener?* inventory in the "Base" column. Record your scores as you retake the test in 30 days. How are you doing? Refine or modify your goals as necessary and repeat the process every 30 days and chart your improvement.

	Base		Month 1		Month 2		Month 3	
	Comfort	Stress	Comfort	Stress	Comfort	Stress	Comfort	Stress
1								
2								
3								
4								
5								
6								
7								
8								
9								
10								

	Base		Month 4		Month 5		Month 6	
	Comfort	Stress	Comfort	Stress	Comfort	Stress	Comfort	Stress
1								
2								
3								
4								
5								
6								
7								
8								
9								
10								

ABOUT THE AUTHORS

Laura Jennings and Olin Jennings were the founders of The Jennings Group, which was located in Columbia, NJ. They provided a broad range of management consulting services as well as training services in leadership development, communication, leading in conflict, leading and managing change, teambuilding, selling, and other interpersonal skills.

Laura has been a management consultant and trainer for over 25 years. She brings special sensitivities and insights on the people side of successful business organizations, strategies, and growth. She also has owned and managed her own executive search firm. She received a bachelor's degree from Drew University and has attended The Institute of European Studies in Vienna, Austria. She has authored articles on such topics as managing people resources and the effective use of management recruiters. She has been a lecturer at the graduate division of Bank Street College in New York City as well as The New School For Social Research, and served as a board member for numerous organizations as well as a professional association.

Olin has been a management consultant and trainer for over 30 years. He also has been in industry for almost 10 years as a vice president of marketing for an office products company, vice president of corporate development for a diversified industrial company, and president of a national environmental services company. He received a bachelor's degree from Lawrence University, a master's in mining engineering from Mackay School of Mines, and an MBA from the University of Michigan. He has authored articles on business issues facing companies including leadership, training, marketing, strategic direction, acquisitions, and other subjects. He has served as a founding director or member of several associations. He has served as an editorial advisor to trade publications and has been quoted as an expert on various markets. He has been a guest lecturer at the University of Southern California business school and Tufts University.

On the personal side, Laura and Olin were marriage partners as well as business partners. They lived on a farm in New Jersey and were weekend farmers. They also raised and showed Labrador Retrievers.

GROWING YOUR INTERPERSONAL SKILLS

Olin Jennings and Laura Jennings are available to work with organizations to improve emotional intelligence, listening and communication, interpersonal skills, and leadership skills.

- Keynote speaker

- Presentations and workshops for management meetings and management teams

- Formal training programs including:

  - ▸ Emotional intelligence - understanding yourself and others
  - ▸ Becoming a 100% listener
  - ▸ Communicating to motivate individuals and groups
  - ▸ Building 3-Dimensional client relationships
  - ▸ Leading change
  - ▸ Leading difficult people
  - ▸ Leading in conflict situations
  - ▸ Enabling others - delegating to empower
  - ▸ Becoming a complete coach and mentor
  - ▸ Selling from *your* comfort zone
  - ▸ Creating a leadership culture

- Personal counseling

For more information contact:

The Jennings Group, LLC
www.TheJenningsGroup.com
Phone: 908-475-1100

Made in the USA
Columbia, SC
28 August 2024

40714099R00061